HOW DOES IT WORK?
CARS

by Joanne Mattern

pogo

Ideas for Parents and Teachers

Pogo Books let children practice reading informational text while introducing them to nonfiction features such as headings, labels, sidebars, maps, and diagrams, as well as a table of contents, glossary, and index.

Carefully leveled text with a strong photo match offers early fluent readers the support they need to succeed.

Before Reading

- "Walk" through the book and point out the various nonfiction features. Ask the student what purpose each feature serves.
- Look at the glossary together. Read and discuss the words.

Read the Book

- Have the child read the book independently.
- Invite him or her to list questions that arise from reading.

After Reading

- Discuss the child's questions. Talk about how he or she might find answers to those questions.
- Prompt the child to think more. Ask: What did you know about cars before you read this book? What more do you want to learn after reading it?

Pogo Books are published by Jump!
5357 Penn Avenue South
Minneapolis, MN 55419
www.jumplibrary.com

Copyright © 2018 Jump!
International copyright reserved in all countries. No part of this book may be reproduced in any form without written permission from the publisher.

Library of Congress Cataloging-in-Publication Data

Names: Mattern, Joanne, 1963- author.
Title: Cars / by Joanne Mattern.
Description: Minneapolis MN: Jump!, Inc., [2018]
Series: How does it work? | Audience: Ages 7-10.
Includes bibliographical references and index.
Identifiers: LCCN 2017027405 (print) | LCCN 2017033281 (ebook) | ISBN 9781624966958 (e-book)
ISBN 9781620319024 (hard cover: alk. paper)
ISBN 9781620319031 (pbk.)
Subjects: LCSH: Automobiles–Design and construction–Juvenile literature. | Automobiles–Juvenile literature. | Classification: LCC TL240 (ebook) LCC TL240 .M363 2017 (print) | DDC 629.222–dc23
LC record available at https://lccn.loc.gov/2017027405

Editor: Jenna Trnka
Book Designer: Leah Sanders
Photo Researcher: Leah Sanders

Photo Credits: servickuz/Shutterstock, cover; photosvit/iStock, 1; risteski goce/Shutterstock, 3; kali9/iStock, 4; Pavlo Baliukh/Shutterstock, 5; Lena Pan/Shutterstock, 6-7; J. Lekavicius/Shutterstock, 8-9; Supit Choosavang/Shutterstock, 10-11; Ivan Kurmyshov/Shutterstock, 12; Dorling Kindersley/Getty, 13 (foreground); TZIDO SUN/Shutterstock, 13 (background); Himchenko.E/Shutterstock, 14-15; Africa Studio/Shutterstock, 16; kpakook/Shutterstock, 16-17; Etaphop photo/Shutterstock, 18; Eric Gevaert/Shutterstock, 19; Jim West/Alamy, 20-21; betto rodrigues/Shutterstock, 23.

Printed in the United States of America at Corporate Graphics in North Mankato, Minnesota.

TABLE OF CONTENTS

CHAPTER 1

CAR PARTS

Have you ever ridden in a car and wondered what made it go? What powers the **engine**? What makes the wheels turn?

Cars are amazing machines. How does a car work? Let's find out!

The most important part of a car is the engine. The engine creates the power that makes a car move.

electric car · · · · ·➤

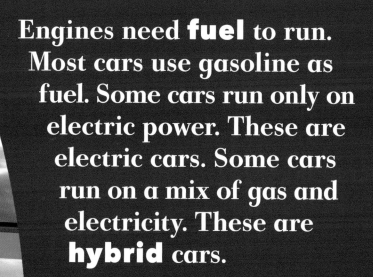

Engines need **fuel** to run. Most cars use gasoline as fuel. Some cars run only on electric power. These are electric cars. Some cars run on a mix of gas and electricity. These are **hybrid** cars.

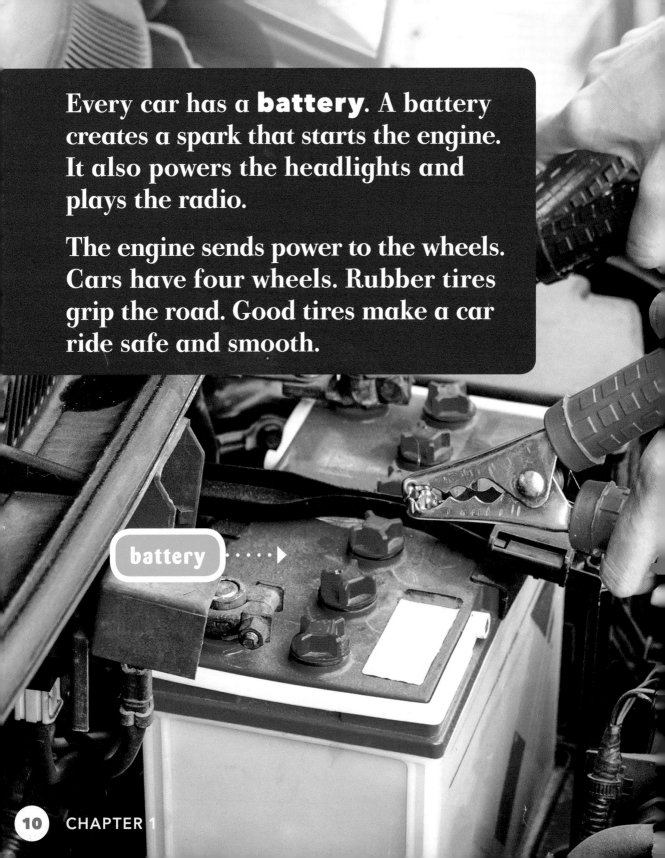

Every car has a **battery**. A battery creates a spark that starts the engine. It also powers the headlights and plays the radio.

The engine sends power to the wheels. Cars have four wheels. Rubber tires grip the road. Good tires make a car ride safe and smooth.

battery · · · · ▶

TAKE A LOOK!

All the parts of a car work together. **Energy** moves from the fuel tank to the engine. The engine sends that energy to the wheels. The wheels move the car.

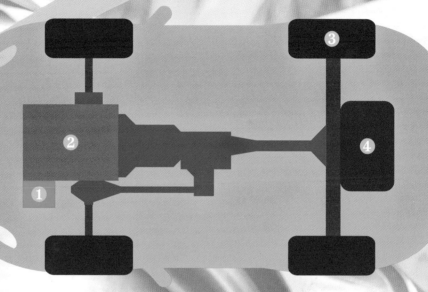

① **battery**
② **engine**
③ **wheel**
④ **fuel tank**

CHAPTER 2

HOW IT WORKS

How does an engine turn fuel into power? It is a process called internal combustion.

Inside the engine, gas mixes with air. A spark plug **ignites** the gas. This creates a small explosion.

spark plug

exhaust

explosion

air

piston

Hundreds of small explosions happen very rapidly. This moves rods in the engine. These rods are called **pistons**. Pistons move the **crankshaft**, which moves the wheels. The crankshaft also connects to the **transmission**. This is what shifts a car's gears. It is what puts the car in drive, park, or reverse.

TAKE A LOOK!

Connecting rods connect the pistons to the crankshaft.

■ = pistons   ■ = connecting
■ = crankshaft   rods

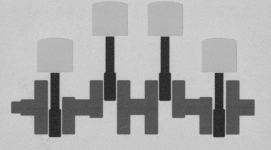

What about when the car stops? Pushing the brake pedal sends a fluid to the brakes at each tire. Discs push against each wheel. This **friction** makes the wheels move slower and stop.

brake

CHAPTER 3

MANY KINDS OF CARS

There are many different kinds of cars. Most cars are made to drive on roads. But some cars can drive off-road. These cars have big tires. They ride high above the ground.

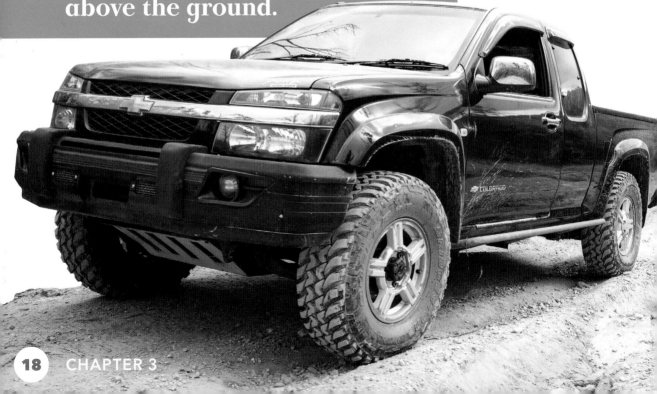

wing ·····▶

Race cars are built to go fast. Some drive more than 200 miles (322 kilometers) per hour! Race cars have big, strong engines. Wings help race cars move quickly.

Today, cars have many **electronic** parts. You can buy a car with built-in wireless Internet. Cars have **sensors** that tell the driver what is going on around the car. These sensors make driving safer.

Engineers work to make cars better. Soon cars will drive themselves. A computer in the car will tell it when to start, stop, and turn. Maybe one day you will ride in a self-driving car!

DID YOU KNOW?

Technology company Google has a fleet of self-driving cars in the United States.

ACTIVITIES & TOOLS

TRY THIS!

FRICTION AT WORK

Friction is the resistance when one surface rubs on another surface. Some surfaces provide a lot of resistance. Some surfaces provide less resistance. How does friction affect a car's speed? Test it out in this activity.

What You Need:

- materials to make ramps (cardboard or wood planks)
- variety of toy cars
- variety of textured materials to create friction (hand towel, sandpaper, dirt, etc.)
- tape
- stopwatch
- measuring tape

1. Construct several ramps out of cardboard or wood planks and differently textured materials. Tape the materials to the surface as needed.

2. Make predictions about how each surface will change the speed of the toy cars.

3. Test the different cars on the different ramps. Use a stopwatch to measure how fast they go. Use a measuring tape to measure how far they go.

4. Were your predictions right? How did the friction of the different materials affect the speed of the cars?

GLOSSARY

battery: A container filled with chemicals that produces electric power.

crankshaft: A long piece of metal in a car that is connected to the engine and helps to turn the wheels.

electronic: Small devices powered by electricity.

energy: Power that is used to operate a machine like a car.

engine: A machine that changes energy into movement.

engineers: People who use math and science to solve society's problems and create things that humans use.

friction: The resistance created when one surface rubs against another.

fuel: Something used as a source of energy.

hybrid: Made of two different things.

ignites: Starts burning.

pistons: Metal pieces in an engine that move up and down to make other parts of the engine move.

sensors: Instruments that detect changes.

transmission: The part in a car that changes the car's gears by transmitting power from the engine to the wheels.

INDEX

TO LEARN MORE

Learning more is as easy as 1, 2, 3.

1) Go to www.factsurfer.com

2) Enter "cars" into the search box.

3) Click the "Surf" button to see a list of websites.

With factsurfer, finding more information is just a click away.